Naked News for Indie Authors
How NOT to Invest Your Marketing $$$

Fully revised and updated (January 2018)
Copyright © 2015, 2016, 2018 by Gisela Hausmann

Published by Educ-Easy Books
via CreateSpace

* * *

ISBN 978-0-9864034-6-0

***

Editor:
Divya Lavanya M.

***

Cover Picture Credit/Copyright Attribution:
Woman's hand with an old magnifying glass by Maisei
Man hands working on the laptop by guteksk7
both via Shutterstock

Twain in his later years (1907) Photographer: A.F. Bradley
This media file is in the public domain in the United States.
This applies to U.S. works where the copyright has expired

***

***

***

***

CONTENT

There are many kinds of authors

- Bestselling authors

- Award-winning authors

- Celebrity authors

- Expert Authors

- Well-known authors

and

- Indie authors!!

This book is written for indie authors and writers who consider self-publishing!

The goal is to help you, dear reader, avoid traps and pot holes, and show you how you can handle many marketing tasks without having to spend a dime.

As you study this book you'll notice quite many illustrations showing you many things I have accomplished. The goal is not to brag but to illustrate that indie authors can accomplish these tasks. There are too many people claiming "pure fiction" which is, in part, what this book is about. The book's other part is explaining the best practices that helped me in scoring these successes.

OVERCOMING YOUR BIGGEST DISAPPOINTMENTS

If you have already published one or more books, undoubtedly you have experienced at least one disappointment that hit so hard that you wanted to give up.

If it is of any comfort – it happens to all of us. The only question is, "Do we find the strength to continue?" Since you bought this book, I know you do, and you are already rolling up the sleeves – again.

Here is one of the most painful and disappointing events that happened to me. I learned a lot from it.

In 2012, I was working an extremely stressful full-time job, which also required doing lots of overtime. Regardless, every evening I went home to work on my book *Naked Determination, 41 Stories About Overcoming Fear*. I also worked through every weekend. It was exhausting, but I was elated and energized, because in my heart I knew that this really cool book would make a difference to peoples' lives. I was sure that all my friends would support me and that they were waiting for my book to come out.

During this period, I had a check-up at my doctor's. He asked me how I was doing, and so I mentioned my book.

"Really?" he said, "Please – tell me everything about it."

He sat down in his chair. Clearly he wanted to hear everything about it, or so it appeared to me. He also asked lots of questions and seemed to get more interested the more I told. Finally, he asked me to inform him when the book would come out because he wanted to buy a copy, plus "one copy for everybody at his office."

In late October, one week after I released my book, I drove by his office to drop off a business card with the information where he could buy my book (just in case he had never heard about Amazon).

The whole week passed without me selling a single book. Obviously he had not even bought one copy.

So, I drove by his office again and dropped off a second card. Having known his staff for a decade, I knew that they would give him the card, especially since I told them that he had asked me to do so.

Again, I did not sell a single book.

Two weeks later, I dropped off a third card, with the same result.

This book cost only $4.99, so his not-buying wasn't about money. The good doc had a very established and reputable office, he drove a beautiful car, and once he had mentioned that all his kids graduated from the most excellent universities in this country.

About six months after publication, on April 19, 2013, my book won Bronze at the eLit awards, 2013. A few weeks later, the local newspaper, The Wilmington Star, featured a very nice article about me and my book, and two weeks after that, I was due for my yearly check-up again.

"Gisela," the doctor burst out as he entered the room, "You won't believe what happened! The other week I was at the hospital and while I was waiting, I leafed through the Wilmington Star. Typically I don't read that paper; I only did because I had to wait there. And, guess what? I saw that article about you and that your book won an award. I immediately bought a copy."

I wanted to burst out, "That's what it took?"

Naturally I didn't, but this was the moment when I learned a very important lesson.

That man who had listened to my lungs and my heartbeat, who knew my blood pressure *and* my weight for over a decade, needed to hear from somebody else that my book is a great book. This somebody did not even have to be the editor of the New York Times Book Review; no, the "authority" of a local newspaper guy, whose articles he never read, could convince him to spend $4.99, whereas I, who he had known for a decade, could not. This was embarrassing and painful to me.

Maybe you understand or even feel my next statement, or maybe you don't.

I, as a human being, felt unworthy, not worth the expense of $4.99, the equivalent of a cup of coffee at the local Port City Java coffee house chain. Of course, all of us are used to hearing from people that they will do this or that and they never do. Consequently, when my doctor did not buy books like he said he would, it was just another one of these events.

However, it turned out that, while my doc was not going to buy a book penned by Gisela Hausmann, a woman he had known for a decade, he was going to buy the book from Gisela Hausmann, the award-winning author, who was featured in the newspaper, IMMEDIATELY. In other words, buying my book was not about me or my book; it was about being in the news. This purchase was not about, "OMG, you wrote a book! How cool is that! I am going to buy it!" It was about, "Oh, maybe you'll get famous; I better buy your book."

In contrast, before I was featured in the newspaper, around the time when I was still hoping that my doc would buy at least one copy of my book, I was contacted by a lady on Twitter. She saw one of my tweets, and tweeted back, "Looks wonderful. Bought it." I did not know her; I did not even know that she existed.

To be precise, then I was befuddled. The many disappointments had weighed heavily on me. I almost could not accept that somebody, who I didn't know existed, was interested in my work. It was this lady's tweet that gave me the boost. It showed me that my work mattered and that there are people who care about books and not possible fame (and fortune). At that time, my book hadn't won the award yet and it hadn't been featured in the newspaper yet. Surprisingly, the doctor, who was a real person in my real life, turned out to be a person with fake interest, whereas the lady in the virtual world of Twitter was a person with real interest.

When we strive to make our mark, we must not allow ourselves to be disappointed by people, whose reactions drag us down. We need to look for and listen to people who lift us up.

So, here are my thanks to Ann Howley, who, with a single tweet, gave me reason to continue. I rededicated myself, entered my book into another award, where it won Gold in its category.

And, Ann? Two years later, Ann Howley published her first book, *Confessions of a Do-Gooder Gone Bad*. It is an awesome book, and I laughed and giggled reading her hilariously entertaining stories. Ann and I will probably never meet, but we are connected through our stories and our will to move forward and impact others in a positive way.

THE NAKED TRUTH THAT LEADS TO THE NAKED NEWS

> *"Twenty years from now you will be more disappointed by the things that you didn't do than by the ones you did do. So throw off the bowlines. Sail away from the safe harbor. Catch the trade winds in your sails. Explore. Dream. Discover."* -- Mark Twain

All of us know Twain's famous quote. It applies to everything we do.

In this case, we can choose to believe that all our friends and acquaintances are only waiting for our books to be released so they can read it. We can also believe that we can buy a Twitter promotion which somehow, magically, will result in hundreds of sales that will lead to our book becoming a bestseller.

And if we do that, in twenty years from now, we might be disappointed that we did not roll up the sleeves and do what's needed to actually help readers discover our books.

I told you the story of why my doc purchased my book because it points to the truth.

People want to be reassured by others that they are making the right decision before they buy.

This fact sounds crazy because we'd like to believe that we have been raised and educated to make our own decisions, that our parents, teachers, and mentors have empowered us to weigh options and take action, like the hero in some Hollywood blockbuster.

Then again, only a few weeks ago, I caught myself doing the same thing. When my son visited for the Christmas holidays, he brought a heavy tome along. He mentioned that he read one or two chapters before going to bed, every evening.

This non-fiction book is currently ranked in the top-400 and also sports more than 2,000 reviews. Since I follow nonfiction bestsellers, I had heard about it but I had not purchased it. My son continued to explain why he liked this book. After he left, I purchased the hardcover edition for almost thirty bucks, the same evening.

*

All these three stories, my doc's, Ann's and my own, have something in common – We listen to others.

As much as we'd like see ourselves like Indy Jones making a snap decision and picking the Holy Grail out of dozens of goblets, we don't. Besides the fact that all of us face time and/or money restraints, we like to listen to the counsel of others.

But, that doesn't mean that this advice is always good, which is what this book is about.

Even worse, when we listen to advice that does not work for us, many of us give up. Which is where Mark Twain comes into play. If we want to succeed, we have to be brave and try new things, again and again, until we succeed. (And if we don't, we'll probably regret it later.)

Every day, I get emails that announce that they'll "reveal how I can automatize my book marketing and achieve my dreams." I am sure you get them too.

The naked truth is that success does not come automatically, but it can be achieved with hard work.

I self-published all my books.

One of them was given to Bill Clinton as a gift (by an Austrian Trade organization).

Another one was featured in Success Magazine and in Entrepreneur.

My work was also featured in one of Bloomberg's podcasts and Bloomberg's Spencer Soper flew to my hometown to interview me, in person.

So, don't let anybody tell you that it can't be done.

But, I worked for all of this and more, and I am sharing my knowledge, naked-ly. You can tell that it's true by the fact that I don't suggest that there is way to become a successful author, automatically.

So, let's get started.

It all begins with the decision between trying to find a publisher or to self-publish.

FIND A PUBLISHER OR SELF-PUBLISH?

When I self-published my first book in 1988, publishing was a whole different industry. Authors who did not want to self-publish had to meet the interests of established publishing houses. Whoever published the book took the risk of ending up with a storage room or a garage full of books. The biggest costs were the expenses for printing and storing the books. Then, as today, large publishing houses, who publish dozens of books throughout the year, needed to keep productions costs as low as possible to reduce their risk.

That is probably the reason why Amazon put so much effort in the development and marketing of the Kindle e-reader; just imagine the warehousing and logistics needs of this largest bookseller in the world.

Today, the danger of ending up with tons of unsold books is gone. Authors can publish in e-book format and also publish physical books via print-on-demand. If a book turns out to be not successful, the financial damage is limited to the costs of

- editing
- cover design
- formatting and
- ISBN number

Authors may be able to cover many of these services with the help of talented friends or hire creative talent at a reasonable cost. Additionally, Amazon, Createspace, Smashwords, and many other Internet publishers offer free ISBN numbers.

Since indie authors may be able to reduce the costs of publishing a book by getting help from friends, they need to examine closely if any publishing company can offer them better.

FACTS TO CONSIDER BEFORE TRYING TO FIND A PUBLISHER

There are *publishers* and PUBLISHERS.

While the quality services of well-known, large publishing houses do not need to be discussed, many different types of publishers who offer various types of "publishing services" are popping up on the Internet like mushrooms after a rain. They should NOT be mixed up with the backbone of the United States' established publishing houses.

Amazon and Createspace belong to this group too. They offer "publishing services" for indie authors but they do not market and promote books like Harper Collins, Simon & Schuster, and Scholastic, just to name a few. However, opposite to vanity publishers and all kinds of other publishers, **Amazon and Createspace do not charge for the services they offer** (though you can buy some services from them).

Like I mentioned before, there are *publishers* and PUBLISHERS.

I too have my own publishing company and you too can set up yours, which is really easy in most US states, especially if you publish e-books only.

Therefore, if you consider finding a publisher to publish your book (rather than self-publishing), it is imperative that you read the wording of the contract you want to sign. Since I am not a lawyer, I cannot give legal advice. However, as a marketing specialist and e-mail evangelist, I recommend reading the **sales pitches** of all publishers with an investigative mind, **before** you even get in contact with any of them.

Here are a few examples:

- No other publisher offers you **more services to help you promote your book** in newspapers, bookstores, and on the Internet.

[*In plain English: YOU have to promote! They do NOT promote, they offer services, for which you may have to pay. In reality, you can find many of these services for free on the Internet, or you can buy them on the Internet without having to pay this publisher's margin.*]

- Your **book will be available at online book retailers** worldwide including Amazon.com, BarnesandNoble.com, and many more online bookstores.

[*In plain English: Thousands of indie authors publish their books every single day at Amazon.com and other online bookstores worldwide. This service is nothing special but the bare minimum.*]

- Book **availability** at iStore, Amazon, Barnes and Noble... John Doe* published with us and ended up with a New York Times Bestselling Book. **Are you next**?

[*In plain English: Again, the fact that a book will be available at these Internet bookstores is the bare minimum. Also, this write-up does not explicitly say that John Doe* really published his NYT bestseller with this particular company. This pitch says "John Doe ended up writing a NYT bestseller." I believe that if the company really published a NYT bestseller, they would have named the title of the book. The final question is rhetorical and does not mean anything.*]

- We have the **expertise you need** to publish your book ...

[*In plain English: World-wide – every single day – hundreds of indie authors, who have never published a book, publish their first book at Amazon.com and other online bookstores. Amazon and all other online Internet bookstores make the process very easy. Additionally, these stores offer free guides on how to do it. Indie authors can also find help in many online forums, from Goodreads to Facebook. Lastly, Amazon's and Createspace's team will help authors. If at any time during the publishing process you have a question, you first check Amazon's or Createspace's excellent Q&A files for answers. If you can't find what you need, you send an e-mail, and within 24 hrs, even the most complicated questions will be answered by an expert.]*

- **Successful book marketing** usually **begins with a press release**.

[*That's only true for celebrity authors. Newspapers no longer publish press releases about anybody else's books. Just open your local newspaper and check if you find any news about any book, other than maybe Michael Wolff's "Fire and Fury: Inside the Trump White House." If your book wins an award or becomes a bestseller, you may get lucky but you'll have to pitch it.*

Successful book marketing begins with having a platform of friends who want to read and review your book as quickly as possible. You should also encourage them to share their reviews on their social media platforms.

Since YOU know when you will publish your book, you can arrange this type of early, social media coverage better and faster than anybody else. Since social media promotion is free, it is probably the better course of action than paying somebody to blast out a press release to journalists who don't care about you, and who are probably waiting for James Comey's new book.]

- **You always keep your copyright as the creator of the work.**

[*Certain publishers have a tendency to describe this fact as if it was a special gift. Just recently I had a budding author tell me quite excitedly, "This publishing company even lets me keep my copyright."*

The copyright is a legal right created by the law of a country that grants the creator of any original work (the intellectual property of artists like authors, photographers, and musicians) exclusive rights to its use and distribution. While there are special situations like writers "working for hire," e.g., for a newspaper or a magazine, in general the copyright is yours just like you are the mother or father of your child. You can sell the right to distribute, just like you can give up your child for adoption, but you will always be the parent of your child.

It is this significant detail that you can sell "the right to distribute" that makes all the difference. If you sell your right to distribute, signing a contract with a publisher means you're agreeing to the terms within; the publisher is now in charge of publishing and distributing your book.

As with any legal contract, the cooperation can be wonderful or can turn into a nightmare. Just ask any divorcee. When he/she signed the (marriage) contract, both parties thought their union would be heaven on earth but eventually it ended in divorce. Therefore, keep your cool when reading certain well-formulated phrases BEFORE you sign! Make sure you clarify what you would have to do if you wanted to get out of the contract (similar to a prenuptial agreement). Then, get the information in writing before you sign any contract.]

Keep in mind that, if, for whatever reason, you change your mind about any detail of your book, the title, the content, or the cover, you'll have to discuss this with the publisher. The publisher may or may not agree to your proposed change. Though, in general, the idea is that because the publisher has more experience than you do, there won't be any need for changes, it happens all the time.

Please don't take my word for it, but go to any author forum (e.g., at Goodreads or Facebook) and ask how many authors have changed anything about their book. You'll be surprised how many authors have done just that, including E.L. James, the author of *Fifty Shades of Grey*.

If you self-publish you own all rights. Should you change your mind about any detail, the content, or the cover, you simply change it. You don't have to ask anybody because all rights are yours. Unfortunately, I know plenty of authors who had to buy back their own book for hundreds of dollars since they were not happy with their publisher's efforts. In all these cases, the contract required them to "buy back" their own book if they wanted to get out of the contract.

AVOIDING TROUBLE and GETTING AHEAD

If you consider publishing with a small (not famous) publisher you owe it to yourself to google the publisher's name and the word "scam," like so:

"...publisher's name" AND "scam."

It's one of the great advantages of our time that we can google facts and snoop around to protect ourselves. So – please, do it!

*

A general rule is – If the "potential publisher" wants to charge you any kind of fee – Hands Off!

Why would they charge you any fees?

Do they believe that your work will sell, or – not?

Are they aware that every day thousands of people self-publish books at practically no cost?

If their answer is that they "need to" charge you for marketing services, please ponder the following. Any successful publisher is making money. Hence, if they are really making money by publishing best books and further book sales by running great marketing campaigns, why do they need *your* money to do it?

The big idea of authors and publishers working together is that authors write because that's what they do best and publishers publish because that's their métier. The concept is *not* that authors finance publishers' business operations.

The other truth is that you can do your own marketing and learn a lot about the industry – information that will help you to

- become a better writer
- win friends and fans (gain a following)
- learn what kind of books your friends and fans want to read
- learn how to market books
- win more friends and fans

… all of which makes you a more attractive author who might get signed on by a serious publisher, in the future.

Today, the best traditional publishers want to meet authors with a big fan community. The immense success of "Fifty Shades of Grey" showed The Big 5 (Hachette, HarperCollins, Macmillan, Penguin Random House and Simon & Schuster) that unknown authors who have a huge fan community can succeed and write a bestseller. Hence – do everything you can to become that author.

*

As you embark on your journey as a self-publishing author,, you might get to a point where you feel, "What happened? I did not sign on with this publisher who wanted eight hundred bucks from me. Why am I am now surrounded by other people who all want money from me. Who should I believe?"

You need to believe *your* own smarts! (Because it's YOUR money.)

Did you ever buy a car or a house? – I am sure that when you purchase big ticket items, you check every little detail. Before you buy a new car, you read consumer reports. Before you buy a used car, you get it inspected by your trusted mechanic. And, before you buy that house that looks like your dream house, you hire a home inspector to make sure it really is.

You can do the same when contemplating the purchase of any kind of book marketing related services.

Though you cannot hire an "inspector" to examine marketing products, you can find out facts. It's relatively easy.

Since practically everything we do on the Internet is being tracked lots of data is out in the open.

Additionally, you can and should ask questions. But, don't ask "everybody," ask your target audience, the people who are most likely going to buy your book.

*

THE BIGGEST FICTION

The biggest fiction of 2017 is that garnering a good number of reviews in reviews clubs, then advertising a book on Twitter, will lead to substantial sales.

This system used to work till around 2016. That year, authors published one million books in addition to the already published 20+ million books, which is an increase of five percent, but of course the number of readers did not increase proportionally. Hence, more authors compete for the attention of the same numbers of readers.

Ask any of your author friends and they'll confirm.

So, what really sells books?

TALK – good, old word of mouth, amplified by social media chatter.

Of course, ideally, you'd have Oprah talking about your book but that's probably not going to happen. So, who else could talk about your book?

- Friends
- Colleagues
- Online friends
- Writer group friends
- Media
- Podcasts
- Blogs
- Guest blogs

really any kind of communication...

Unfortunately, as explained in the opening chapter, even some of your friends and acquaintances will begin to take your work seriously only when "others" talk about your work...

Now you might say, "Which others? I am talking to "others" all day long but they aren't buying my books and not all of them are spreading the word."

Remember Ann? When Ann tweeted that she bought my book, I didn't know that Ann was writing her own book, that she was interested in other books that told autobiographical stories. Ann responded because in contrast to my doc, she was really interested in finding story books.

To find others who want to buy our books and also spread the word, we have to identify our target group of readers as precisely as possible.

Whereas tweeting to "everybody" will return limited results regardless whether you do it yourself or you hire somebody to do it for you, speaking to your specific target audience will get results. This includes the media.

As mentioned, my work was featured on Bloomberg. However, it wasn't featured in the book review section but by the reporter who writes about "everything Amazon," including Amazon reviews. Even within the same organization not "everybody" will be interested to spread the word about our books.

THE IMPORTANCE OF REAL RESEARCH

I studied mass media at the University of Vienna; among the many theoretical exercises we students had to do, one stood out. A professor asked us to envision a situation in the fifteenth century, when only one book existed – the Bible. The Bible was the first book that got printed on Gutenberg's printing press.

In the 15th century, this only book was _not_ the only form of mass media. Wandering theater troupes entertained people, rich and poor. However, before books were mass produced (instead of being copied by hand), poor(er) people had no way of acquiring _entertainment_ and taking it home. They could only remember what they had seen and heard and tell others about it.

Naturally, then as today, people want _to own_ items that entertain them, in the furthest sense of the word. That's why we buy the books and videos we buy and why we record moments we want to remember, forever.

Supply & Demand

Because people want to own entertainment, printing presses were a rousing success. By 1500, more than twenty million books got printed and during the 16th century an estimated 150 to 200 million copies. Soon, all over Europe, people could choose what kind of book they wanted to read.

This situation literally exploded in the 21st century because today everybody can also publish their writings.

In other words, the original situation, "only one special book for everybody who can read" turned into "millions of books for fewer people than the ones who can read." Today, people choose to acquire entertainment in different formats.

That's why today's self-publishing authors need to market their books to the specific readers who want to read their specific books.

*

My university courses covered this topic as well; my professors' answer to all related questions were two words – data collection and statistics.

Most artists do not like to hear these two words. They sound boring and everybody knows that doing this kind of work is boring. Still, it is more important than ever. In this century, every influencer hoards data; but, if it's flawed it doesn't help.

Flawed Data

A well-known example of flawed data collection is the US presidential election 2016.

Based on the data she saw, Hillary Rodham Clinton thought she'd win. Maybe even Donald Trump thought she'd win and certainly most reporters thought she'd win.

The reason was – most of them looked at the same flawed data. HRC's team did not examine the "real data" from the Rustbelt states, the voice of voters who eventually helped Donald Trump win the election.

*

Authors looking at "flawed data" means pursuing "everybody", including people who prefer to *watch the movie made from the book*. Asking fellow authors about their opinions of books they would not buy also leads to collecting flawed data.

In contrast, zooming in and learning about your real readers' preferences will help you in designing everything from the book cover to your marketing campaign.

Here is how it matters:

As I am writing this book, I am already testing three potential covers for this book. Obviously, the target group is indie authors. So, I posted three potential covers to Facebook author friends, asking them to pick their favorite.

*

After 24 hours, 48 authors had weighed in. 18 male authors and 30 female authors. That's approximately 37% of male respondents and 63% female respondents.

Overall
27% liked cover #1.
56% liked cover #2.
16% liked cover #3.

Though the choice seems to be clear, there is more to this topic than we can see at one glance. Best data research requires more effort than adding up numbers and figuring out averages.

Of the 30 women:
5 had voted for cover #1, which equates to 17%.
23 had voted for cover #2, which equates to 77%.
2 liked cover #3.

However, the 18 men voted very differently.
50% liked cover #1.
27% liked cover #2.
33% liked cover #3.

Though the female authors had a clear preference, the male authors did not necessarily go along with it.

What was to be learned from this?

To make a best decision, we need to examine industry trends as well as personal data.

My **personal data** included the fact that previous editions of this book had been reviewed by twice as many women as men.

Important industry information from reputable organizations instructed that in 2017 "Women Rule in Indie Publishing." Here is one of the many articles.

https://www.publishersweekly.com/pw/by-topic/industry-news/publisher-news/article/73469-the-indie-publishing-feminist-revolution.html

Hence, I did not have to run a complicated data analysis to figure out that I needed to give preference to the opinion of female authors (77% liked cover #2) which was also supported by 27% of men. Also, notice that two times as many female authors responded to my query which supports the article's findings.

*

In short: This is not complicated math. You can do this too!

Most artists shy away from collecting data because they have heard that it takes a lot of effort, creating control groups, and complicated analysis; hence, they don't do it at all.

While for the longest time this may have worked it doesn't work in this market with about a million books getting published per year.

So, if you write Sci-Fi, ask only readers of Sci-Fi books for input. If you write steamy erotica, don't ask people who read Christian romance but only people who read erotic romance.

*

Even if you have absolutely no designer skills, you can select pictures from the Internet, smack your title over it in MS Powerpoint and use these very basic layouts to survey your target group.

*

Knowing "real data" is important even if you hire an award-winning cover designer because YOU need to tell them WHO your audience is. If you survey your target group, you can send your designer a basic layout and request, "a cover like this, only 'MUCH better.'"

Here is an example that might explain this issue better.

About half a year ago, I read a travel book that sported an award-winning cover from a multi-multi award-winning designer.

I myself am a world traveler who has traveled forty-seven countries, hence the book seemed like a great fit; the stunning cover was an appealing invitation to buy it.

Before I purchased the book, I also looked at its 30+ excellent reviews; everything I saw and read seemed to suggest that I would love this book. Alas, I didn't. It turned out that the book's relatively young author had written a book for an audience of younger people who just wanted to travel.

The book didn't really describe the people and/or locations the author visited. Instead, it elaborated on all kinds of information younger people might want to know. I gave it three stars and was pleasantly surprised when the book's author thanked me for my input.

Even though I had given the book (only) three stars, I recommended it to two young people because I thought and also said so in my review that the author's elaborations on how she financed her long trip were excellent. Though I personally wasn't interested in this information, I knew it would help the two young people.

I also believe that if the author would have picked a great travel picture of herself, she'd probably sell more books. The stunning award-winning cover is a work of art, but it does not reflect, "Hey - that's me, only 20+ years old! I made my dream come true! I traveled to foreign countries and this book tells you how I did it."

The current award-winning cover advertises the book to #travelers (like me).

A *better, maybe more successful* cover would attract:

#YoungTravelersWhoHaveADream
#YoungTravelers
 #TravelersWhoDontHaveMuchMoney

And, that's one example why every author needs data collection and evaluation.

*

At this point you might say, "Well, it's easy for you to talk. You write authors' books, there are authors everywhere."

That's true but you can always look for input in the "right venues."

In 1998, long before Facebook was invented, I published my early childhood education book "obvious LETTERS." Then, I surveyed parents and teachers in public schools, Montessori schools, and I even visited three synagogue schools.

Before I released my book "NAKED WORDS: The Effective 157-Word Email," I spoke to business people because business people get drilled about the importance of personalized emails by business magazines.

Naturally, I also made mistakes.

Before I released "NAKED WORD's" student edition "NAKED TEXT: Email Writing Skills for Teenagers," I spoke with students and parents of college bound teenagers. Eventually, after I released the book, it turned that though many parents thought it was very important that their children learn best email writing techniques they did not rush to buy my book.

Though such revelations are unpleasant, this is not a time to be frustrated and give up, or keep advertising to the vast group of "everybody." It's the moment to get more data!

I kept on researching and asking question. Finally, one-and-a-half years later, a very blunt lady told me, "It's not *my* job to buy all books that would help my child, the school needs to do it. Your book should be in every school and college library."

Ahh... yep, why hadn't I thought of this?

I immediately changed course and began marketing this book to libraries. It turned out that even though the book's professionals' edition was featured in Success magazine, librarians were more interested in buying the student edition. Though quite obviously I had not thought about it, librarians know that professionals buy their own books whereas parents and teachers rely on them.

*

So, if you too realize that your data might be flawed data, stop doing what you are doing and start asking your target audience questions. If you ask enough questions, some "very blunt people" will give you the answer you were looking for.

Everybody collects flawed data from time to time, but that does not mean that we can't start over collecting more, better, or newer data, change book covers, advertise to different groups, and so on.

COLLECTING AND INTERPRETING DATA

In the 21st century, collecting and interpreting data is an integral part of business. Everybody knows that Google, Amazon, and Facebook are doing it all day long.

Though none of us can run these corporations' complicated operations, basic data collection is quite easy.

Most importantly – Always be patient!

You would never buy a house or a car spontaneously because you want to base your decision on real facts. It's the same for buying marketing campaigns.

As a general rule: Always follow the potential provider for at least one week.

TWITTER ADS (basic action pattern)

Follow Twitter ads the provider is running. Specifically, follow the promotions of books from your book's genre _and_ subcategory. Monitor three to five books the ad provider is running and record these books' sales numbers for at least five days

Fictitious example:

Monday morning	#1,110,000
noon	#1,200,000
evening	#500,000
Tuesday morning	#115,000
noon	#68,000
evening	#91,000
Wednesday morning	#67,000
noon	#100,000
evening	#80,000

Thursday morning	#160,000
noon	#180,000
evening	#230,000
Friday morning	#440,000
noon	#415,000
evening	$470,000

Even if you are only starting out and don't know how these sales ranks convert to book sales, this data tells you something. Maybe the ad campaign did not sell enough books to recover the costs of the ad but clearly this fictitious scenario shows sales of a quite a few copies.

On the other hand, if a book's sales rank drops/improves only once during five days, clearly, the ad campaign isn't working.

*

The fastest way to record sales rank numbers is to bookmark the books you are following on your Smartphone and set your timer to ring every eight to ten hours. Whenever it goes off, you pull a screenprint of the sales rank.

A better way that helps you gain more useful data for the long run is to record the sales ranks of various books from various providers on an Excel spreadsheet for more than one week. If you record sales rank data multiple times throughout the year, you'll be able to figure out which provider might deliver best results for you.

In short – Don't ever be impressed by sheer numbers, always look for specific numbers.

The Statistic Portal reports the following numbers given by Americans when answering the question "What types of books have you read in the past year (2015)?"

47% Mystery, thriller, and crime
33% History
31% Biographies/Memoir
27% Romance
26% Cookbooks
26% Science Fiction
24% Fantasy
23% Classic literature
22% Health and Wellness
20% Religion and Spirituality
19% Self-Help
19% True Crime
13% Political
13% Current Affairs
13% Graphic Novels
11% Business
9% Poetry
8% Chick-lit
7% Westerns
30% other fiction
35% Other non-fiction

Still, if you buy a Twitter ad from a book promoter with 100,000 followers, you have no guarantee that your ad reaches 9,000 readers of poetry. Or, 26,000 hobby cooks.

Recording and evaluating actual numbers will help in getting better results. If you buy ads from a promoter with a specific, targeted following, you may be able to attract the interest of a higher percentage of this promoter's followers, like 20% tweeps who are interested in poetry or 50% hobby cooks.

Sometimes, buying an ad from a promoter with a smaller list may yield better results if this promoter's following happens to be your specific target group.

Like they say, "Numbers don't lie" but you need to know that you are looking at the right numbers.

To get best insights also check the engagement level of Twitter promoters' followers; they may have up to 50% inactive followers.

Again, this is easy. You can audit Twitter accounts at these three websites:

https://www.twitteraudit.com/
https://www.socialbakers.com/
https://fakers.statuspeople.com/

Summing it up: Naturally, checking numbers takes effort BUT that's how you make the data work for you.

Lastly, you can check the results of your tweet campaigns, who supports you, and all your data on Tweetreach(dot)com.

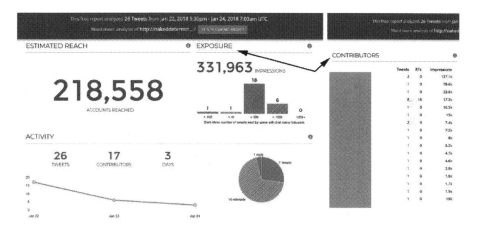

The following illustration shows that having a supportive fan community who know your work and are willing to help is the best help for indie authors ("virtual word of mouth")

I was able to reach more than half a million Tweeps without buying a campaign:

My Snapshots

All
Purchased
Last 7 Days
Last 30 Days
Older

http://smarturl.it/5ggf0k
As of October 31, 2017 at 01:02AM UTC
100 tweets reached **528,163 people** with **901,695 impressions**.

ONLINE MAGAZINE ADS

Researching best online magazines for placing ads follows the same pattern as researching Twitter promotions.

Study the magazine, see how many people "liked" the magazine issue and how many people commented on it. Then, check out the magazine's ads and follow the sales ranks of books that are featured in these ads.

PRINT MAGAZINE ADS

All print publications from magazines to newspapers ought to provide you with their readers' demographics. If you contemplate purchasing an ad in a print magazine, just google "name of publication AND reader demographics" to find data sheet like this one.

https://www.forbes.com/forbes-media/wp-content/uploads/2015/06/2016-PrintDemographics.pdf

Even your hometown newspapers as well as local radio stations and TV stations can give precise data.

FACEBOOK

Unfortunately, it is quite difficult for indie authors to gauge Facebook promotions.

Authors have the option to buy ads from Facebook themselves or buy a promotion from a book promoter. In the latter case the promoter features a book posting on their page which is fed in the news stream of its followers.

Still, on average, not even sixteen percent of promoters' followers get to see these postings because most detrimental to indie authors' marketing efforts, Facebook really has three feeds (News feed, Pages feed, and Explore feed).

Promoters' postings on Facebook pages most often end up in the Pages Feed but most authors and their followers don't even know how to access it.

Secondly, individual followers may be following too many pages or have set their individual settings in a way that will keep them from seeing the promoter's postings.

Facebook is a complicated turf for indie authors and small business owners. For more information please see my "The Little Blue Book for Authors: 101 Clues to Get More Out of Facebook."

BLOGS (WORDPRESS)

Since most bloggers engage in Content Marketing, few of them sell ads.

As always, it makes sense to see how many readers "like" and "comment on" individual blogs.

EMAIL AD CAMPAIGNS

Just like with Twitter followers, the number of subscribers does not matter as much as how many subscribers open the emails and buy books.

The naked truth is that you'll never know real numbers unless you create your own email data base.

In contrast to newspapers, TV and radio stations, I don't know of any provider who'll give you "actual numbers" of opening rates.

That's why everybody wants to create their own email list because that's the only way to really know facts.

Though your own list may be smaller, it contains only names of people who really want to follow YOU, hence most likely the opening rate is higher.

Example:

A book promoter has 10,000 email addresses in their data base. At least, 3% of subscribers open the emails and buy books.

3% of 10,000 equals 300.

Your own list holds only 250 email addresses.
45% of subscribers open your emails and buy books when you offer a special deal.

45% of 250 equals 112.

In other words, even though the marketer's email list holds almost 50 times as many addresses as your own list, buying a campaign would lead to only three times as many sales.

If the marketer promotes more than one book in the same email, the 300 sales may have to be split between a few authors.

Also, the cost of the campaign have to be factored in. If you offer a 99 cents deal, 200 additional sales will return an extra $68.00

YOUR OWN DATA

Finally, be aware that other people will try following your data just like you can follow everybody else's trail.

Considering how many books are being published, many reviewers and bloggers are trying to find out if authors are serious about becoming an author. They will check out your profile to see how vigorously you promote your book and if other book bloggers have already reviewed it.

To improve your chances to get these influencers' attention, save every feature in which your book "starred" – blogs, guest blogs, newspaper articles, TV appearances, and of course a link to Amazon and Goodreads reviews.

Here is how to save blogs properly:

On the day the blog gets featured, capture the individual blog URL and save it in a personal database.

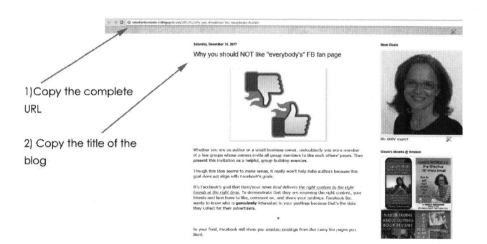

In this featured example the specific blog URL is

http://nakeddetermination.blogspot.com/2017/12/**why-you-should-not-like-everybodys-fb.html**

In contrast, the *blog's URL* is

http://nakeddetermination.blogspot.com
The blog's URL will always display the latest blog. It could change two to three times per week.

Specific blog URLs never change, which is why it is so important to make them part of your book's representation on your website.

Once you have saved the specific blog URL, you can post it at social media sites, email it to your friends, and of course you can also email it to potential book reviewers to demonstrate that x number of book bloggers have already decided to feature your book in their blog.

But why stop there? You don't really want to put too many links into an email; a much more professional way to present this type of information is to create a 'newsroom' at your website. This newsroom displays all blogs, newspaper clips, video interviews, and TV-interviews in which you and/or your book are featured.

Possible titles:

- 'Newsroom'

- 'In the News'

- 'Featured in the Press'

This is how your 'newsroom' could look like; there are no boundaries to your ingenuity and creativity.

Once you have created it, use your 'newsroom' as an asset!

Actively offer bloggers that you will link from your website to their blog and ask them if they have a logo they want you to use. If they don't have one, build one by

- creating a screen print of the blogger's website,

- pasting the screen print into a powerpoint slide,

- saving the powerpoint slide as a jpeg,

- trimming the jpeg to an attractive logo (keep in mind that all logos should be the same size),

- placing the logo on your website and linking it to the individual blog URL.

If you update your newsroom continuously, it will serve as an impressive portfolio.

Though this method takes some effort, it has major benefits:

a)   You'll never lose a blog address.

b)   Creating this 'newsroom' enables you to send proof that your book has been chosen, featured, and reviewed at many blogs via a *single link* to a single website. You can write to potential reviewers.

"… My book has already been featured at various blogs. Please find more information at (yoursite).com/(newsroom).html …"

Since it is not easy to get important bloggers' attention, be creative when you approach bloggers. Consider which bloggers might have an interest in featuring your book. If your book's genre is

love story > historical fiction > Italian

your book will appeal to bloggers who blog about

1. Romance,
2. History, and
3. Italy.

Thus, you could also approach travel bloggers who write about Italy, send them a few pictures of the region in Italy where your book plays out, and ask if they want to review your book. Equally, you could contact bloggers who blog about romance and relationship issues.

IMPORTANT: Make sure that you own the copyright of all pictures you send to others or use pictures from the CC0 Creative Commons, Free for commercial use.

One of my books, *Naked Determination, 41 Stories About Overcoming Fear*, features quite a few travel stories from all over the world.

Trying to be creative, I approached a few travel bloggers. Relatively quickly (within 24 hours), I found two travel bloggers who were extremely excited to feature my book. Travel bloggers do not get asked for book reviews or author interviews too often; thus they do not have a long reading list. Many of them enjoy reading a book with great travel stories. Therefore, they post much faster.

Did you notice something?

By getting exposure for my book that features travel stories on travel bloggers' sites, I was speaking directly to people who really like traveling.

Obviously, not everybody does. Again other people don't care to read about a globetrotter's adventures because they themselves prefer to book comfortable, guided, luxury trips.

However, by promoting in venues for travelers, I was able reach people who eventually wrote in their reviews,

> *"... Her love of travel, zest for life and determined spirit shine through the prose..."*

> *"... My favorite is her adventure to Tibet. If she had waited, she would not have seen the Tibet she longed for, rather the new and modern Tibet with a train that leads to it. The author got to ride with chickens, experience old style motels where everyone shares a toilet and there's no heat. But she got to see the Tibetan building she dreamed of, all red from the morning sun and she even includes the picture!..."*

"... She traveled to Russia, Mongolia and China during the iron curtain days and the chapters about those are good to read. The reason being these days we have the TLC, Natgeo and online travel guides which help us to plan for a foreign locale. However during the cold war era flow of information was restricted and it must have taken enormous amount of courage and a bit of craziness..."

Yep, these readers appreciated my "craziness" and for that I am immensely grateful.

Though I can't know for sure, I don't think that my doc would or could have written any of these passionate lines.

*

So, that's your #1 reason why you should zoom in on your target audience. The people who care about what you have to say will share their feelings with others and on Amazon.

YOUR OWN DATA IN THE HANDS OF GIANTS

Obviously, not only can every blogger follow your data, the biggest data hoarders on the planet can follow it too. And, they do.

One of these data hoarders is Amazon.

In 2015, I published "NAKED TRUTHS About Getting Book Reviews." As a top reviewer whose email address was listed on Amazon and also an award-winning email evangelist, I saw what authors needed to do to improve their odds of getting their books reviewed by Amazon top-reviewers.

The book was a rousing success. Alas, of the 26K authors who looked at the book, many did not buy it. Thousands opted for following the ideas of owners of review clubs who suggested "We help each other and review each others' books."

This is a scenario where data hoarding plays an enormous role. Amazon, the data hoarder, could measure the results of these activities in real time.

Let's say, in a certain month, 10,000 authors decided to review each others' books. Club members from various clubs reviewed an average of five books in a particular month. That's 50,000 book reviews that Amazon hosted but did not make a dime on the sales because the authors gave each other the books for free.

That's also 50,000 reviews of which many may have been "inflated" because review club members have a tendency of giving each other favorable reviews. Amazon, who has the duty to upkeep a review platform that lives up to the standards of the FTC's truth-in-advertisement laws, not only did not make any money on these transactions, but also had to worry about these reviews' integrity.

And, they did!

First, Amazon made it mandatory that reviewers who received a free book had to identify themselves as having received a free book.

A few months later, they installed a drop-down menu that enabled their customers to see at one glance how many verified reviews and non-verified reviews books received.

And, finally, they disconnected the top reviewers' email addresses, thereby robbing indie authors of the opportunity to contact the very people who wrote the reviews that customers appreciated the most.

At this point it looks as if Amazon might even do away with non-verified reviews altogether.

Certainly, had all these indie authors decided to invest in my book, I would have made some nice money. Also, some authors who, by objective evaluation, have sub-par writing skills would not have received any reviews at all. BUT – let's look at the bigger picture of things.

Within less than three years, indie authors went from *"access to thousands of excellent reviewers"* who, for free, wrote seven paragraph reviews, which many authors consider better reviews than Kirkus' reviews, to *"no top reviewer availability, at all."*

That's the effect of data hoarding and having the capability to analyze this data with the help of algorithms. In the 21st century, nobody can outrun a data hoarder, least of all, Amazon! They know things we can't even guess.

As described in the previous chapter, you can create a fabulous news room. Maybe, book bloggers who check it out will read every blog that was written about your book and maybe they won't. Maybe, they'll just glance at your webpage, be dazzled and accept your book.

But, that's not what happens at Amazon. Amazon reads numbers, every day, maybe even every hour. If, in a certain month, they register the posting of 50,000 to 100,000 non-verified reviews which did not help them to make a dime, somebody is thinking about what to do about it. This situation will be discussed in staff meetings, and somebody will take action.

Obviously, there is very little anybody can do about this now. Though I am sure that most authors would love to again have the old scenario from 2015, when about 5,000 of the 10,000 top reviewers accepted indie author books for review, we cannot turn back the times.

Then again, knowing that one can't outrun data hoarders may help in avoiding mistakes in the future. Spreading awareness about the results of data hoarding will help.

HOW DO YOU GET THE ATTENTION OF THE MEDIA?

Naturally, another great way to find more readers is to have your book mentioned in the media, in magazines, and on TV. It's a particular good route to take for nonfiction authors, children's book authors, but also authors who write books that fit to a specific holiday. For instance, the media likes to hear from romance authors before Valentines and from horror book authors before Halloween (for obvious reasons).

Begin by deciding on your greatest strength:

- Do you have a fabulous voice that will make radio listeners love you?
- Does the camera love you and you love TV?
- Are you a master of the pen, who likes to phrase and re-phrase?

Play into your greatest strength and approach radio hosts, TV-hosts, newspaper and magazine editors, and top tier bloggers as you see fit.

One of the best resources for authors is HARO (Help-A-Reporter)

https://www.helpareporter.com/

If you are not subscribed, you should do so immediately.

- Go to Subscriptions,
- scroll down to
- Sign Up Today and
- "Start Pitching Journalists on topics they want to hear about."

HARO will e-mail you information about what kind of stories journalists, bloggers, other authors, and radio and TV-hosts are working on.

All you need to do is to pitch your angle.

Aside from HARO, you can pitch any editor you like. This is the 21st century, the century of unlimited communication.

To get the attention of media persons:

1. Read as many articles from the media person of your choice as you can. If they are on TV – Watch their shows!

2. Follow them on Twitter

3. Share their tweets/material/news

4. Comment on their articles or blogs

5. Don't use a template but communicate in your own words. Most media people have a degree in journalism or related studies. They can spot a template faster than you can say "template."

6. Finally, pitch your best idea!

Pitching means you devise a plan for a story and send it via email.

It is important that you do not "advertise" your book. All media outlets make money by selling ads but they don't run free ads. So avoid to imply that you want a free ad.

When media outlets feature your work they will be happy to mention your book but not as an ad but rather as your credentials.

Obviously, nonfiction authors pitch a topic that is related to their expertise. The author of a cook book would not pitch their book but something thematic, like, for instance

- "7 Soups, perfect for hot summer days"

Fiction authors need to be a bit more creative. The author of a romantic novel could not pitch her novel, but something thematic, like for instance

- "Valentine's Day is coming up, 5 Romantic traditions from the Middle Ages you have never heard about"

or

- "June is the most popular month for weddings. Local romance author shares 7 tips to plan a wedding most effectively"

*

Some authors are hesitant to approach the media. They are worried that their pitch isn't good enough or too far out the ball park.

Don't be worried!

The media is constantly looking for good stories and NEW stories. The sky is the limit, especially now that every media outlet has to compete for the attention of viewers/readers with hundreds of other outlets.

Also, media persons aren't out to give you a "D" or an "F." They merely look at your idea to see if it fits for their audience and that's it. If you pitch them often enough you'll get your chance.

Important: Once they feature you, return the favor and blast their news clip or article to all of your followers repeatedly, so their clip or article is getting shared often.

BRAD PITT AND I

I once pitched a TV station about a news event involving Brad Pitt. I know you are raising your eyebrows right now because you can't imagine that I know Brad Pitt. And – I don't. However, that does not mean that I could not pitch a topic related to Brad Pitt.

What had happened was that Brad Pitt, who had played Heinrich Harrer in the movie *Seven Years in Tibet*, had tweeted on the Chinese version of Twitter that he wanted to visit China. But Pitt was banned from entering China because of his starring role in that movie, which the Chinese government did *not* appreciate as much as the American viewers.

How did all this relate to me and my book?

In my book *Naked Determination*, I tell the story of how I had met the real Heinrich Harrer, who was Austrian as I am, and how Harrer personally had encouraged me to visit Tibet. I had followed his advice and visited Tibet in 1987. I had even visited the Dalai Lama's former bedroom, where he and Harrer had many discussions before the Dalai Lama had to flee into exile.

The pitch was easy, "Brad Pitt wants to go to China where is he banned from entering… People want to know what's going on… Local author Gisela Hausmann can explain…"

While all of this may sound far-fetched to you, of course it isn't to me, because it is material from my book. I had met Harrer, I had traveled Tibet, I had watched the movie, and I was able to *connect the dots*, and therefore – I am a qualified expert who is able to talk about this topic.

Equally, you can connect many dots about your topic, which I know nothing about. And, that makes you an expert, ready to be an expert guest on TV.

At this point you may be thinking, "She has easy to talk; she writes non-fiction."

The system is the same for fiction books, too. Did you know that there are 56 Renaissance fairs that last at least two weeks, in the United States? There are also Renaissance fairs in Canada, Australia, and Europe. At the time when these fairs happen, every TV station close to the cities where the fairs take place would want to hear from an expert who can talk about "How authentic the jousting events are" or "Why even today people are still fascinated with that historic time period" and dozens of other related topics.
There also Science Fiction conventions (World, National, and local), Horror conventions (World, National, and local), Comics and Popular Culture conventions and so on.

Lastly, somebody else may create an event or a reason, which you can use to pitch your local media; just like Brad Pitt did for me, and he does not even know that I exist.

When *Harry Potter* became the rave, TV stations needed experts who could talk about magic and ghosts. Then, I saw a news feature with a lady who talked about "How to host a Harry Potter-Hogwarts party." And, when *Fifty Shades of Grey* became a bestseller, you can guess which experts were qualified to talk about that topic (a lot of people who never thought that their specialty would be talked about on prime time TV).

Your benefit of being featured on TV, or in any print media, will be that your name and the title of your book will be listed at the bottom of the TV or article. This leads to face recognition ("I have seen him or her, she/he was on TV") and name recognition. People will begin to recognize you as an expert. People like to buy books from experts.

As you go along, you'll see what works and what doesn't, and you'll get better. Before you shell out $1,000 to $2,500 for a publicist, you might as well try this route, which doesn't cost anything. This way you can save your marketing budget for things you can't do yourself. All it'll takes is figuring out your pitch and sending a well-crafted e-mail to a news anchor or a magazine editor.

CONTACTING MEDIA PERSONS

Sometimes, it seems that even though authors like to write they experience writer's block when writing emails. Many authors don't seem to be able to "get themselves in the right mood. "

Here is one way how to do it:

1. Pull up an empty word document, meaning – start from scratch!

2. Reduce the document's size so it covers only about 3/4 of the width of your screen and place the document either on the right or left side of your screen, whichever "feels" more comfortable.

3. Search for and save the portrait of the media person you want to contact or a person you truly respect (many of these portraits can be found on Linkedin.)

4. Place that picture in the upper corner of the *other* side of your screen and reduce its size so it does not overlap your word document. This will allow you to type while also keeping the portrait visible on your screen.

5. Then, type your request email and make your case.

6. Imagine that you are explaining to this person who you don't know too well but who you respect why they should feature you on TV.

7. Every time you get stuck with your writing look at the portrait. If indeed you were talking to this person you would know exactly what to say.

8. Keep your email concise! Aim for about 150 words or a screen-ful. If the recipient needs to scroll to see the whole email they'll "feel" that it is not concise.

9. Save the document. Do NOT send the email right away!

10. The next day, pull up the document and the portrait again and re-read the email "to the respected person (the portrait on the screen)."

11. Does it sound good? Edit the email if needed.

12. Finally, personalize the email by adding the reviewer's, the blogger's, or the media person's name and voila – you probably just wrote a perfect email.

DID YOU DO THE MATH?

So far we have examined how you can save time by self-publishing your book instead of spending maybe years to find a reputable publisher, while at the same time making yourself a more attractive author to be signed on by a reputable publisher in the future.

We have looked at how you can save money by advertising in the venues that will most likely yield the best results for you.

And, we have explored how you can get media coverage without having to hire an expensive publicist. Especially, the latter will yield terrific results for you. You can "reuse" media coverage on all social media platforms to affirm that you are an author who is going places. Make no mistake – that's what your followers want to hear.

Everybody would like to read the next "hot" author's book first; everybody wants to spread the news about an upcoming author.

Of course, all of this is going to take work; then again, success never comes easy.

Overall, it is indie authors' biggest problem not to fall for solutions that look good but won't get you anywhere.

So let's examine which other "temptations" for wasting time or money lie in your path.

LEARNING FROM CONTENT BLOGGERS

Blogging is not only a respected art form, it is also a content marketing tool. Blogging at least once per week helps content marketers to stay in touch with their existing clients, win new clients, and sell product or services.

But it's only effective when the blogger cares enough about the reader to research the topic and provide valuable information.

Blogging is new, but content marketing has been around for more than 100 years; one of the early examples is the Jell-O marketing campaign of 1904.

Even though Jell-O has been sold since 1899, originally, it didn't sell well in stores. American housewives didn't know what to do with it. Finally, the Genesee Food Company who owned and distributed Jell-O placed an ad in Ladies' Home Journal offering "free bestseller" recipes. The campaign was an instant hit. The fact that housewives didn't have to figure out how to prepare delicious Jell-O desserts did the trick.

More recently, content marketing is being used by experts like lawyers, cover designers, and editors to explain to potential customers how they will benefit from using their more expensive services.

For instance, though most authors have at least some working knowledge about the copyright, very few know how to proceed if their copyright is being infringed. The blog of a lawyer who has handled actual copyright infringement cases will deliver helpful information.

*

The problem begins when bloggers choose topics they don't know too much about.

For instance, quite often I see indie author blogs about procedures to get book reviews from top reviewers or book bloggers. One of these blogs contained two traps that probably led to all top reviewers ignoring these requests.

The author-blogger suggested to begin the request email by stating something like "I found your name on the list of Amazon top reviewers."

Problem #1: These are useless filler words.

How do I know? I really am an Amazon top reviewer. Since it takes at least two to three years of steady reviewing to become a top reviewer, it is wasted words telling a top reviewer how indie authors find us. We know.

Problem #2: Too many authors don't edit their emails for personal appeal.

The mentioned email seems to suggest between the lines, "I don't really care what books *you* like. Since you are a top reviewer I hope you will read and review *my* book."

Making this error is detrimental to authors' efforts. Top reviewers read books because they enjoy reading and reviewing books, not because they want be used as unpaid marketers.

Obviously, this second problem only arises because the blogger suggests mentioning the top reviewer's status.

It is difficult to mention somebody's special status and then pretend that this status has nothing to do with why one person contacted the other.

If, in this case, the indie author would focus only on presenting their book to a person who is known to enjoy reading this particular genre the problem would not even come up.

Hence, following this blog's advice hinders indie authors in succeeding instead of helping them.

*

So, what can blog readers do to avoid acting upon incorrect information?

1) Remember the First Amendment
When reading a blog always remember that in the United States the First Amendment guarantees people the right to write, even about things they know nothing about or can't prove to be true. Therefore:

2) Check the blogger's background & the blog's publication date!

Every blogger features a short resume at the beginning or the end of their blog. Always study it; if need be—verify it.
If a blog is older than six months, chances are at least some parts may be outdated. Things change quickly these days.

3) Do the math!

It's easy. Just ponder what will happen if 1,000 authors follow the exact same advice.

As a practical example:
A blog suggests that authors should contact reviewers who read their book's genre with an email that begins with the words, "I found your name on the list of Amazon top reviewers." or "Hi, I saw that you reviewed (title of book). I just recently published a book that is similar..."

Then, imagine that you are a reviewer who receives 1,000 emails that all start with these same words. What would you think upon receiving the fifth email?

Would you think "How wonderful"? or would you think, "OMG, Why don't these authors use their own words?"?

If you evaluate all blogs by the "1,000 people rule" you won't waste time and you'll achieve much better results.

OTHER FREQUENTLY PRESENTED TIPS

"... TO SUCCEED YOU NEED TO FIND A PROFITABLE BOOK NICHE..."

This statement sounds intelligent, but the truth is that nobody knows what a profitable niche is.

Before *Harry Potter* was published, virtually nobody discussed books about young magicians. Before *Fifty Shades of Grey* was published, many people could not name five elements of sexual practices involving BDSM.

Thus, please do not focus on such statements; instead listen to the people who know:

"Write what you know." – Mark Twain

Mark Twain did, and so did J.K. Rowling and E.L. James. Even better – the creation of their books created profitable book niches. That's because readers like new ideas and concepts.

"... GET AS MANY REVIEWS AS POSSIBLE..."

The number of reviews and sales rank of a book should correlate.

As a general rule, a book that has been on the market for about three months should have half-a-dozen reviews. That is an achievable goal. Everybody has at least six friends and acquaintances – in real life and at social media platforms – who read books. If this is a hurdle for you, you need to put down this book and start writing a list of people who are probably interested in reading and reviewing your book. Do not spend another dollar on any book promotion until your book has at least six reviews. Instead, pick up the phone and call somebody. You can and should ask people to read and review your book; you just cannot ask them to lie about how they liked it.

As an Amazon top reviewer, I also believe that about a dozen of well-written reviews represent the majority of opinions any reader could arrive at. I don't know anybody who reads more than a dozen reviews to make up his mind whether he should purchase a book or not. Therefore, if your book has a dozen reviews, you don't need to try to get more. If, instead, you promote your book at social media platforms — for free — you'll put your time to better use. You'll get your book and your cover out (name recognition) and you'll sell a few books. By attracting more readers, you'll increase the chances that you'll get reviews organically.

If, for instance, you wrote a novel about a mystical hunter, you will achieve better sales results if you try to get your book into the bookshops of hunting lodges or into any social media forums for hunters. Inevitably, people who like to hunt and also like to read will buy your book. These people know other hunters and will spread word about your books to this niche group of people who like to hunt and to read. Contrary to that, book reviewers may like your novel but most likely they won't know too many people who hunt.

The basic idea of getting as many reviews as possible is that the numbers of reviews is supposed to convince the potential buyer that this book is a well-liked and well-selling book. Getting as many reviews as possible alone is not going to do the trick. For example, if a book has been reviewed 100 times but has a sales rank of #900,000+, no potential buyer will believe that this book is or was a bestseller.

Quite to the contrary, the disparity between the number of reviews and sales rank will make buyers wonder "Why?" and "What's going on with this book?" In contrast, a book with sales rank #900,000+ and 40 reviews looks as if the book sold very well in the beginning and eventually experienced a sales slump (which is a normal occurrence). Readers are intelligent people; and readers, who read a lot, have a pretty good concept of Amazon's sales rank system.

"… LIST A GIVEAWAY ON GOODREADS AND EVERYBODY WILL START TALKING ABOUT YOUR BOOK…"

If you are already a published author with a large following, this may be true; however, if you are a newbie, most likely it won't.

Readers on Goodreads learn about your book when it shows up in their newsfeed. For instance, if 100 people, who have an average of 100 friends each, enter your giveaway, the "news" that they entered the giveaway will show up in the feed of their combined 10,000 friends (100 x 100). Seeing this information in their newsfeed gives the 10,000 friends of the original 100 friends the opportunity to also enter your giveaway. All they need to do is click on the displayed link.

However, in reality, 5,000 of these 10,000 people may not even log into Goodreads for a few days. By the time they log in, the news about your giveaway will be buried among dozens of other news. 3,000 of these 10,000 people may not enjoy reading your book's genre, and 1,000 others may not be attracted by the cover etc.

Thus, this general statement that just listing a giveaway will create interest is simply wrong.

Additionally, since January 2018 listing a giveaway will cost you money. Hence you want to plan your giveaway thoroughly so you'll get the best return. The ultimate goal needs to be to befriend as many people as possible who are *really* interested in your books, in helping you, and talking about your book.

If you can accomplish that Goodreads is the best venue to market your book effectively. The social media platform for readers has now 65 million members who care about books and authors, and who like to read.

With a bit of luck, almost all winners of your giveaway will review your book.

That's when it gets interesting. Every time one of the readers who reads your book posts an update about how many pages he read and possibly even adds notes, this information will appear in the newsfeeds of his followers and friends. If you know readers who read your book, you could encourage them to post updates.

This is what it looks like:

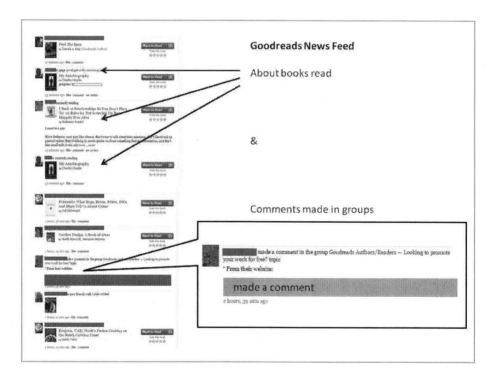

Naturally, the more often your book shows up in the newsfeeds of readers the more they'll be inclined to read your book because apparently "everybody else" reads it. Additionally, if they click the cover they will see that they already marked it as "Want to read."

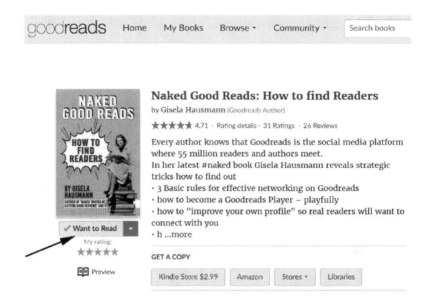

Also, every time one of your friends makes a comment in a group, this comment will show up in your newsfeed, as well as in the newsfeeds of all his other friends. That information is important, because it'll tell you who among your friends is active and engaged. These are the people you should make friends with.

What if you don't want to scroll through your entire newsfeed to find the comments?

Click – "Groups" in the bar at the top of any page at Goodreads – check out "My Groups" (meaning your groups) – click the link to any of your groups. In the header of the group page will be an "edit"-button right next to the words "You are a member." Click it and scroll to the very bottom of the page to find a link that says "edit group discussion updates." Click that and set the settings to "Notifications only."

Once you do that, all comments made in your groups will pop up under notifications (please check the following picture). This gives you an opportunity to study all comments to see who is active and engaged.

Additionally, if readers' Goodreads accounts are linked up with Facebook, Twitter, or both, the news updates will show up there too. That is significant because this is how news about your book will be spread to other social media circles.

In the above illustration, you can see how I marked the progress I made with reading a book, and how this information shows up in my social media feed at Facebook and Twitter.

Lastly, on Goodreads, you can post other information – videos and blogs. Anything you post will show up in your friends' and followers' feeds. If enough of them see your postings and like them, everybody will start talking about you and your book.

Have you noticed something?

All of this is FREE!!

To get noticed on Goodreads stands in direct correlation to your own efforts to get noticed.

Firstly, you have to make friends. Only your friends will see "your news and updates" in their feeds.

Therefore, make friends! Goodreads offers dozens of tools (like the Goodreads widget) to attract new friends. Participate in Goodreads discussions and befriend the readers who share your interests and views.

[Please note: Again, it does not make sense to befriend *everybody* because the people who don't share your interests and views won't enter your giveaways and won't like your comments. Therefore, they won't do anything which will be shared in their friends' feed.]

In order to be successful on Goodreads, you have to participate and be an active member of the community. If you follow these steps and eventually list a giveaway on Goodreads, everybody will start talking about you and your book.

SPEAKING OF FREE...
WEBINARS AND VIDEO SEMINARS

You don't have to hang around in Facebook author communities for very long to see ads for free webinars and video seminars about self-publishing, getting publicity, and learning how to become a paid speaker pop up in your newsfeed. Facebook collects the information that you are an author (because you are a member of author groups) and shows you these ads.

Most of the seminar hosts promise to show you tricks to sell thousands of books, to get on Oprah's TV channel, and other related marketing concepts.

These free seminars aren't really seminars, they are TEASERS!

If you ever inquired about the price of Facebook ads, you know that they aren't cheap. Most likely, any organization who pays for displaying their offerings prominently on your Facebook feed wants to recover the costs of these advertisements and earn some more.

Therefore, in their free seminars the hosts are not going to tell you everything you need to know, but hint about options, opportunities, and possibilities. The seminars offer some value, but to get all information, you'll have pay.

It is important to know that these teasers should to be understood as a chance to learn *something*; they are not "samples," like a sample from a cosmetics company or a free food sample at your supermarket. The effect of the latter two will last only for a short time, but taking teaser seminars gives you an opportunity to learn 10% to 15% of a skill you can build on.

Which is why I do not want to discourage you from taking some of these teaser seminars, BUT I want to you to listen with the mindset of Sherlock Holmes, and I encourage you to apply best practices for attending teaser seminars.

As always, there are *seminars* and SEMINARS. The better the seminars are, the more expensive they will be.

However, no matter how good or bad the seminar is – eventually YOU'll have to do the work. They won't!

That's because you bought a seminar and not services.

Depending on your budget, it may make sense to buy one or more of these seminars, as long as you realize that seminars are the equivalent of going to school. In school, teachers teach you how to write an essay or a business letter but when, eventually, you are out there, writing a business e-mail to a business partner, it's you who needs to do the work.

The only way you can find out if you can really profit from buying a certain seminar is by

1. listening and not getting carried away
2. taking notes
3. examining your notes
4. checking if the host is a copy cat
5. thinking it through

and, possibly, do all of that – again.

Always attend the webinar or seminar with the mindset of a detective conducting an investigation. Most of these seminars are trying to get you to focus on your wishes and feelings instead of applying logic. The hosts want you to buy "something" eventually; they will not present "naked" facts.

In my book *"BOOK MARKETING: The Funnel Factor: Including 100 Media Pitches,"* I describe a pretty foolproof way to get on local TV and I also offer 100 pitches buyers can use. If you pitch your local TV-station correctly, your odds of succeeding are excellent.

On the other hand, even though I have heard dozens of presenters say that with the "right pitch" *anybody* can get on Oprah or *"Good Morning America,"* that is not true. In reality, the opportunity to "pitch the right pitch" may never come up.

Firstly, even if you live in a big city like Chicago, the numbers of *local* expert authors who want to get on one of the *local* TV-stations is limited; also local TV-stations are on 365 days per year, which implies that all (local) Chicago authors can get their chance.

In contrast, there is only one "Good Morning America"-show, on which most authors from the *entire* United States would like to appear. Clearly, the odds of succeeding are worse.

Secondly, even if you are booked to appear on *GMA,* a news event like a terror attack could "interfere" with your actual appearance. On the day after the tragic 2017 Las Vegas shooting, no TV-host was going to present a "sweet" topic; everybody focused on the tragic events in Vegas. Any authors who might have been scheduled to talk about any kind of topic aside from terrorism got "rescheduled until further notice."

Thirdly, unless you are a natural, which very few people are, you have to learn and practice being on TV and hence my suggestion to practice "being comfortable" on local TV where the standards are less rigid than on national TV.

Still, while trying to get on local TV is an excellent "career step" in many ways, if you live a 90-minutes drive from the next TV station, you will face additional challenges. You'll have to stay overnight at a hotel to be focused and looking your best at 6:00 a.m. the next morning.

Since I write "naked books" I present this information in my book. Typically, webinar and video seminar hosts do not. They assume that you will do everything and anything, which may be required even if in reality it may be difficult and/or costly to do so.

Here is another example: If you live in Alaska, you'll have to fly to New York a day earlier if you were to appear on *GMA* because the time difference works against you. That poses additional difficulties if you want to pitch a "current event" pitch.

In short: To come up with a plan you can execute successfully, you have to keep logistics in mind.

Also, though many of these webinars begin with somebody saying how they bought a seminar at a time when they had maxed out their credit cards and how the seminar helped them to become hugely successful, I do not recommend that you do the same to find out if a certain seminar's promises hold up.

Here is how to find out if the webinar or video seminar might help you:

1. When attending webinars and video seminars, **listen *closely and do not get carried away***. If you can, ask questions. The more details you learn, the better you'll be able to see the complete picture. Never throw logic out the window! For instance: To make *their* case that *their* seminar is a good deal, almost always hosts will promise you "lifetime access" to their course. While *they* will live up to that promise, it won't do *you* any good; in the last twenty years, the publishing industry has undergone more changes than in the preceding 500 years and this trend is bound to continue. Whatever the course will teach you will be outdated in a few years.

2. **Take notes**!! Here is one of the easiest ways to this:

- Plan to watch the seminar on your desktop!
- Pull up a word document BEFORE the seminar starts
- Focus! (Turn off background music and don't play solitaire while listening!)
- Take screen prints of every slide you get to see!
- Copy and paste the screen prints into the word document!

This sounds easier than it is done. Naturally, the hosts of the seminars know that you can do that so they will present many slides in rapid succession; you will have to be fully focused to copy and paste all of them in time.

3. **Examine your notes**. Never buy a.s.a.p. at the end of the seminar but always examine your notes and

4. **Beware of copy cats**! – Seminars aren't a new thing. I attended my first one in 2004, but of course, they have been around much longer. Over the last few decades, some of the people who took these seminars seem to have decided that running their own seminars is most profitable. They may be people who never made it onto Oprah or GMA. Whereas the original creators of the seminars have actually done the things they say hundreds of times, many of the copy cats may have only dabbled in the subject matter. They may not be 25% as qualified as the original creators.

How do you find out who is who?

Investigate, on Google! Don't confine yourself to looking for "words," look for pictures and videos, too!

Here is an example to illustrate the concept thought:

with George Foreman   with Armin Mueller-Stahl   proof

In one picture I am depicted with heavyweight champion George Foreman, in the other one with Oscar nominee Armin-Mueller-Stahl, who got famous for playing Cardinal Strauss in "Angels & Demons."

The naked truth is that I met George Foreman for fifteen minutes on the occasion that he received my first book, in 1991. A friend who knows I'm a big boxing fan, and who worked for the company that gave Foreman my book as a gift, arranged that I could meet him in person.

However, I know Armin Mueller-Stahl much better. I was the production manager of a movie in which he starred, a few years before he got nominated for an Oscar. For nine weeks I saw him every day for more than ten hours. When the whole team had to stay at a country hotel, because we were shooting at a remote location, he entertained the team every evening with funny stories from his illustrious career.

Looking at the two pictures on the left, you can't tell how well I know the two men. However, there is also proof of what I just claimed – my first book and a picture from the movie shoot.

All three of these pictures were shot before the digital age began. Even back in the "olden days" people documented important events. Today, people shoot pictures and take videos all day long, which implies that you should be able to find proof of everybody's claims of accomplishments.

5. **Think through everything!**

- From a logistical standpoint: Can you execute the tasks with very few difficulties; if not, how much *extra* money and/or time will it cost?

- Do you have personal handicaps, and if so, are you willing to overcome them? As an example, I was born in Austria. English is my second language and I speak with an accent. Even though I have been a guest on more than a dozen radio shows, I never felt I was doing well. Finally, I adjusted my strategy. I don't try to get on radio shows any longer. I have found out that I feel much better being a guest on TV where viewers can *see* me speak; my accent is less of an issue. Please note that I tried to not to feel flattered that I could make it onto radio shows. I examined what I did and said to myself, "You are never at your best because you don't feel comfortable. You did it a dozen (actually 13) times but you can't distance yourself from worrying about your pronunciation. Leave it and do something that works better for you!" – And, that's what I did... [Now, if I had a voice like Meryl Streep, that'd be a whole different story.]

- Brutal honesty works best. If you took notes, examine them closely, and think through everything with brutal honesty. That will help you to know what is best for YOU!

Webinars and video seminars are a great way to learn new skills but you have to pick wisely.

What if you are not sure?

Sometimes, learning a new skill involves so many unknown factors that you just can't be sure if you can execute what the course teaches. In such a case, try to do what the *free* teaser seminar taught you. Stay subscribed to the host's mailing list and re-take the free seminar when you have more experience with what it'll take to execute the whole program. You can repeat this process as often as you like until you can make the best decision for yourself.

USING BOOKSCAN DATA TO YOUR ADVANTGE

Indie authors need to take advantage of the Nielsen BooksScan data.

While frequently authors get into discussions on whether it is better to publish paperback books with CreateSpace or IngramSpark, or both, almost always this debate is incomplete.

In general, the biggest advantages of both publishers are the following:

CreateSpace delivers with lightning speed in Europe, so if you expect to sell books there, you should publish with CreateSpace. In the days of one-click purchases, most people want to receive their goods quickly.

Whereas CreateSpace prints only paperback books, IngramSparks also prints hardcover books with jackets. If your book lends itself to be given as a gift (e.g. children's books, poetry books, business books et al.) you should consider publishing with IngramSpark. Additionally, IngramSpark is the preferred vendor of bookstores and libraries.

Therefore, typically, indie author debates end on "if you want your book in libraries and/or bookstores," you should publish with IngramSpark.

Here is why this debate is incomplete:

Bookstore buyers but also library buyers order based on two criteria:

a) publicity and
b) the Nielsen BookScan

The US Nielsen BookScan lists sale numbers of "paperback and hardcover copies" by US state and regions within. It is being published weekly. It does not list e-book sales because it was created to help bookstore buyers and the media. If a book seller does not report to Nielsen (e.g. you yourself selling books at a speaking engagement), sales won't show up in the Nielsen BookScan. Nielsen estimates that they report approximately 85% of all print book sales in the US trade retail market.

Considering how many books are being published today, bookstore buyers and library buyers don't have the time to read blurbs and make judgment calls of if and how many copies they should buy based on what they read. Also, fluctuation can be huge.

For instance, in the months preceding a royal wedding, sales of books about royals, weddings, and related topics will climb, but shortly after the wedding they'll fall back to the average sales numbers. After a tragic event like a terrorist attack, books from known antiterrorism experts will climb the sales ranks rapidly, which makes it clear why news and publicity are major influential factors for bookstore buyers.

Of course, there are also trends which are less easy to spot. For instance, a new food trend might emerge in New York City, on the East Coast. Slowly but surely the trend spreads and people begin buying this type of trendy cook book at a steadily increasing rate.

A bookstore buyer from a small city somewhere on the West Coast (far away from New York City) who doesn't cook himself and/or doesn't read articles about emerging food trends won't know about this development. Then, one day a customer might walk into the bookstore and ask for a cooking book featuring recipes from this new trend.

After taking the order, our fictitious bookstore buyer will look up the Nielsen BookScan. Seeing that the book is selling extremely well on the East Coast, he'll probably not only buy the one copy for the customer but also stock a few extra copies.

What does that mean for self publishing indie authors?

If you publish steamy romance novels, which generally speaking most readers read on e-readers, your book's BookScan score may never get high enough for bookstores to stock your book.

If you write reference books for professionals, most likely more people will buy the paperback edition of your book and your book's BookScan score will be higher, automatically.

If you write nonfictions books for authors like I do, the results will be mixed, because authors are used to reading books on e-readers.

The good news is Amazon shows your book(s) BookScan results on their Author Central page. Here is one of mine.

Though there are hundreds of factors that will influence book sales, this map illustrates an interesting scenario. Looking at this BookScan map, you can see one glaring "white spot on the map," the state of Utah. Considering that people in all other regions of the United States buy physical copies of my books, it seems somewhat surprising that not a single copy has been sold in the relatively large state of Utah.

One explanation might be that my brand is built on publishing naked (no fluff) facts. While surely Utahns appreciate the concept in general, maybe they don't appreciate the titles I chose.

[*Naked* Words, *Naked* Text, *Naked* Truths, *Naked* News...]

As of 2012, more than 60% of Utahns are counted as members of The Church of Jesus Christ of Latter-day Saints. I don't know if they consider my calling my brand "naked" inappropriate. Then again, maybe there is another reason which I just can't guess. In essence, it really doesn't matter but I probably should not advertise or plan a book signing tour in Utah.

Naturally, you can influence your book's BookScan scores. You can ask your friends nationwide to order your book in bookstores and improve your score this way.

The other way to influence your score is to seek the attention of the media.

That's the route I chose. My book *"NAKED WORDS 2.0 The Effective 157-Word Email"* got featured in SUCCESS magazine (print edition). If you check the map, you'll see that I sold the most books in regions where lots of entrepreneurs live and work: San Francisco, CA, Los Angeles, CA, Chicago, IL, Minneapolis-St.Paul, MN, Cincinatti, OH, Houston, TX, Raleigh-Durham, NC (the Triangle), Philadelphia, PA, and New York, NY.

However, the region where I sold most books is the Greenville, SC region, where I live. This can be explained quite easily: Over the last eight months, I have been a guest on WYFF-4, my local NBC station, five times.

You can also see that I sold books all the way to Atlanta, GA where many Greenville residents have friends and relatives. Probably, quite many people told their friends, "Guess what, I saw this author on TV. She wrote a book about writing best e-mails..." Even being on local TV gets the word out.

People can watch TV or not, but if they watch, they can't scroll away. Equally, people who already spent a few bucks on a magazine probably take the opinions and recommendations of the editors seriously.

Summing it up: Being in the news will get your book into bookstores and libraries regardless of where you publish your books, CreateSpace and/or IngramSpark.

DANGEROUS WORDINGS

Promotional programs, tools, or products can be the biggest expense for any indie author. Like almost every author, you too probably receive between one and five sales pitch e-mails per week. If you want to avoid spending money unwisely, **study the wording** of the sales pitch e-mails carefully.

You can recognize sales pitch e-mails easily because they follow an established pattern.

1. Typically these e-mails feature **white background** only
2. They begin with **raising expectations** and **reminding you of personal wishes and dreams**. The idea is that you'll focus on your emotions rather than put your analytical skills to work.

   "Would you like to get a whole lot more sales..."
   [*Who wouldn't?*]

   "Are you where you want to be or..."
   [*Yes and No! While we should be grateful for what we have, there is always room for improvement. Therefore, this is a rhetorical question.*]

   "Do you want to see your book on the New York Times Best Seller List one day?..."
   [*Who wouldn't?*]

3. After one or a series of questions, the e-mail will **describe the program or product** the sender wants to sell in a few paragraphs. Between these paragraphs, you'll find **testimonials** of previous graduates of the presented program or buyers of the product.

4. Lastly, the e-mail will suggest that the program or product is worth an X amount of money (which you have no way of verifying) but if you "Buy Now," you'll get the program or product at an immensely reduced price, which could still be higher than what you considered to be a reasonable price. Very often, a bit of research might reveal that you can buy a book that covers the same topic for only a few dollars. The senders of these e-mails know that, which is why they incorporate lots of action calls like "Buy Now" or "If you buy today," so you make your decision quickly.

[*This is a standard pattern for all self-help programs regardless of whether the program creator offers a weight-loss program, indefinite riches, or anything related to book promotion. (Some of the programs are good; but too many are not.)*]

*

"... With this system, you can write a book in a weekend..."

[*While this may be true, what kind of a book will it be?*
Also, how long will the editor have to work on it?]

"Easy reading is damn hard writing." – Nathaniel Hawthorne, novelist of *The Scarlett Letter*.

*

"... Turn your writings into strong passive revenue..."

[*"Passive income or revenue" is the income which is received on a regular basis but requires little effort to maintain it. For instance, earnings from a rental property could be passive income and so would be earnings from a book you wrote years ago.*

The thing with it is, you can't just "turn" your writings or book into strong passive income. In life, there is no turn sign to "Success Road," anywhere. Only work will get you there. Even people who inherit stocks or properties need to watch the stock market and maintain the properties, or they have to pay somebody to do it. And, as all of us know, not even that is a fool-proof system because some employees or contractors fail.]

*

"… Learn how to turn 30+% royalties into 70% royalties…"

[There is nothing to learn. Amazon will offer you to choose between two royalty options: a 70% royalty option and a 35% royalty option. Additionally, the royalty options also depend on in which country you live in, in which countries you sell books, and lastly into which Amazon programs you enrolled your book. But, whatever your choice is, Amazon will offer you these options without you having to ask.]

*

"… Easily double your Kindle book sales with only 45 minutes of work …"

[I'll admit this concept thought had me baffled for a second. The writer(s) of this statement are suggesting that publishing your Kindle book also on Createspace will double your book sales.

There is no evidence that this would happen and I would guess that no single book sells an equal number of e-books and paperback books. Different readers have different needs. People who read a lot read mostly e-books, because it's cheaper. Environmentalists read mostly e-books to protect trees. Certain reference books sell better in paperback form because they may be used by multiple users in one office or company. Therefore, this is a misleading statement. I also addressed this subject in a previous chapter.]

*

"… Enroll into… xyz… seminar TODAY! For the first time in history, we'll bring together…"

[*Really? "For the first time in history?" These are mighty big words. How does anybody know these days what is happening for the first time in history when it is happening at a seminar?*]

*

As you can see these pitches are all about words. Some of these words are chosen to make you think that you'll receive something special, which it is not.

So, how can you find out if the program, tool, or product is a good one?

TESTIMONIALS ARE KEY TO FINDING OUT SOME OF THE NAKED NEWS

Here is how you can <u>analyze</u> testimonials.

Note down the name of every author who gave a testimonial. If the author has a common name, you should also save his picture; there may be more than one author by that name.

Then, go to Amazon.com and search for the author and check out the ranking of every book he published.

Lastly, you also need to check when the author's book(s) were published. In the last fifteen years, I have seen the same testimonials over and over again, even though the author has not published a new book in years. Therefore, it is important to check the publication date because some types of promotions worked beautifully in the past but don't work any longer. For example, promotions on the radio used to be big. Meanwhile, satellite radio has been invented and podcasts have become the rave.

Repeat this process for every author whose testimonial was featured in the e-mail. I know, this is annoying legwork, but would you rather spend thousands of dollars on a hunch?

I promise you'll be amazed with the results of your research. More than likely, you'll find that many books of the authors whose testimonials you read are ranked worse than your own. (But you haven't spent any money on these programs yet.)

Testimonials and pitches are all about words. Since you are an author, you love words; and, you think about words. Therefore, you won't have the slightest difficulty in maneuvering through this jungle of words; all you have to do is to shut off wishful thinking and evaluate what a particular phrase really means.

"… After every radio interview, I get a huge spike in my author ranking and my Amazon sales have more than doubled… "

[*Not informative! Doubling means "times 2." In an extreme case, it could mean sales doubled from 1 book per month to 2 books per month. If this author's book would have reached bestseller ranking, he probably would have said so.*]

So, why are authors like this one giving testimonials for a program if it did not help them reach bestseller status?

They are being told that giving a testimonial is one more way to get their name out, which is true. Additionally, no program offers authors to get sales results; they always offer to teach participants certain skills. Unfortunately, there is a problem with this.

Not everybody will learn every skill easily. For instance, though I am a savvy home improver who has renovated two houses built in the sixties (including remodeling two complete kitchens), my tactile skills do not extend to repairing cars. I have never ever changed a tire in thirty years, even though logic would say that changing a tire has to be much easier than renovating a complete kitchen, including installing new floors, cabinetry, granite-tile counter boards, backsplash, and lighting fixtures, as well as painting the walls and the ceiling.

Naturally, if I was stranded in the desert and my cell phone did not work, in other words, if my life depended on it, I'd still attempt to change a flat tire. Even if I had never read a manual on how to change a tire, I would try to figure it out. If faced with certain death, I'd probably succeed because when we are faced with certain death, most of us can accomplish things we never dreamed of doing.

However, in reality – None of us is faced with certain death if we do not succeed in turning our book into a bestseller!

All of us want to achieve that, but do we wish for it and work for it hard enough – in the same manner as if we were stranded in the desert with a not-working cell phone?

While I know my own answer to this question, I don't know yours, but since you are reading this book I am guessing – You have set mind on pushing your book as far as it can go!

~~*~~

AWARDS

Another huge topic in indie author circles is whether authors should enter their books in award competitions, or not. Once, I saw a remark in an online discussions which stated, "Authors who won an award think that awards help them and the ones who don't say awards are not important."

It isn't that easy anymore. There are hundreds of thousands of books being published every year. As of today the five Pulitzer Award winning books of 2017 received an average of 1,008 reviews on Amazon, which becomes less impressive if one knows that "The Underground Railroad: A Novel" by Colson Whitehead (Pulitzer Prize Winner)(National Book Award Winner)(Oprah's Book Club) received 3,879 reviews, whereas 2017 Pulitzer Prize Winner in Poetry "Olio" by Tyehimba Jess received only 15 reviews.

*

Since I write "naked (no-fluff) books" I am not even going to pretend that winning an award is easy.

Even the most talented writers face one problem which is – The market is flooded with books. Today, on average, 1,500 books are entered in pretty much all reputable book awards but only one book can win, in each genre. Those of us who enter awards know that occasionally, we are torn about what we wish for, probably like the actors who are nominated to win an Oscar.

In 2015, I entered my book "NAKED TRUTHS About Getting Book Reviews" in the Kindle Book Awards, genre Non-Fiction. The Kindle Book Awards feature only seven categories:

- Literary Fiction
- Non Fiction
- Young Adult (YA)

- Romance
- Horror
- Mystery/Thriller
- Science Fiction/Fantasy

First, the committee nominates 20 books in each category that receive Semi-Finalist Badges. Out of these 20 books 5 Finalists are being chosen, and finally, 1 winner in each category.

In 2015, the year when I entered my book, John Brooks' book "The Girl Behind the Door: A Father's Quest to Understand His Daughter's Suicide" won the Non-Fiction category; my own book was a Finalist, *only*.

What can I say? Of course, I wanted to win. What else? But, when I checked out the other Finalists against which my books was competing Brooks' book stood out, immediately. I had known people who had committed suicide.

And, that's why I knew that my book shouldn't win.

In a way, I actually wanted Brooks to win. Because his mission was really important.

Things like that could happen to you, too.

In a way, it is almost unavoidable. Many great books are getting published and authors aren't shy about entering them in awards. And, since there are only so and so many reputable book awards, our books are bound to lose against other books, in a certain year. It's the same as in any other industry.

One of my favorite actors of all times, Peter O'Toole was nominated for an Oscar an astonishing eight times, and never won. Finally, in 2003 the Academy awarded him with an Honorary Oscar for his contributions to the film industry. Sir Richard Burton was nominated seven times and actresses Glenn Close and Deborah Kerr six times. Neither one of them won an Oscar.

That's life. So, if you don't win that's what you have to tell yourself.

Now, getting toward the end of this book you might say, "Ghee, Gisela Hausmann, I love this book... I value what you are saying, namely, "You have to work it"... but aren't there any shortcuts on the road to success?"

If you are a good writer but not a good marketer, indeed, there might be one.

THE BEST WAY TO GET RID OF ALL MARKETING PROBLEMS – START SMALL

Publishing a book was always a huge endeavor and it still is. The fact that today everybody can publish their books themselves doesn't change a thing, in fact, it might be making things more difficult.

If you just like to write and don't want to engage in marketing too much you could turn around and start small again.

You don't have to publish yourself or try to find your way through a jungle full of traps.

There are literally hundreds of writing competitions that you can enter by paying a small fee of 12, 20, or 35 dollars. Many of them offer cash prizes and some offer publishing contracts.

Below is just a taste of what's available. Please google your genre to find hundreds of other writing competitions.

Now, keep in mind, almost all of these competitions ask for unpublished material. So, if you decide to go this route you can't brag about being an author, you'll be a writer again. However, you can make yourself a name *the safe way*. You might even win a couple of thousand dollars along the way.

You could do what many writers long for:

Hide behind your desk and write. In fact, the more you write, the better. Most of these competitions ask for shorter pieces. You could take a break from publishing books, focus on writing four to five short pieces, and enter each in a different award. In a year from now you could have a publishing contract with a reputable publisher or possibly been chosen for writer's residency.

Australian Book Review
Annual Calibre Essay Prize
Prize: $5,000, the winning essay will be published in ABR's 400th issue in April 2018.
Deadline: January 15, 2018
https://www.australianbookreview.com.au/prizes-programs/calibre-prize/current-prize
*

Hidden River Review Trilogy Awards: Non-Fiction, Poetry and Very Short Fiction
Prize: $1,000
Deadline: February 28, 2018
http://hiddenriverarts.wordpress.com
*

Tor House Prize for Poetry 2018
Prize: $1,000 for an original, unpublished poem not to exceed three pages in length.
Deadline: Postmark March 15, 2018
http://www.torhouse.org/prize/
*

Essay Collection Competition
Cleveland State University Poetry Centre
Prize: $1,000, publication, and a standard royalty contract
Deadline: March 31, 2018
http://www.csupoetrycenter.com/essay-collection/
*

Nimrod Literary Awards
First Prize: $2,000 and publication
Genre: Fiction, Poetry, Short Story,
Deadline: April 30th, 2018
https://nimrod.utulsa.edu/awards.html
*

Tom Howard/John H. Reid Fiction & Essay Contest
Prize: $2,000 each for the top story and the top essay. The top 12 entries will be published online.
Deadline: April 30, 2018.
https://winningwriters.com/our-contests/tom-howard-john-h-reid-fiction-essay-contest
*

Fellowship of Australian Writers NSW Inc.
3 Sutherland Shire Literary Competitions
Traditional verse, Free verse, Short story
Prize: $1,000, an additional 'Shire Resident's Prize' of $250 may also be awarded at the judge's discretion
Deadline: April 30, 2018
http://www.sutherlandshire.nsw.gov.au/Community/Library/Sutherland-Shire-Literary-Competition
*

Bristol Short Story Prize
Prize: £1,000
Bristol Short Story Prize will publish the 20 shortlisted stories in both print and ebook formats in association with Tangent Books on October 13th 2018
Deadline: May 1, 2018
https://www.bristolprize.co.uk/rules/
*

Writer's Digest Annual Writing Competition
Grand Prize: $5,000 in cash, an interview with the author in Writer's Digest, one on one attention from four editors or agents, a paid trip to the ever-popular Writer's Digest Conference, and more...
Deadline: May 4th, 2018
http://www.writersdigest.com/writers-digest-competitions/annual-writing-competition
*

Palooka Press Contest
Short fiction
Prize: Publication by Palooka Press (a perfect-bound book with a glossy color cover), $300 honorarium, 20 free copies of the book
Deadline May 15, 2018
http://palookamag.com/palooka-press
*

The Emerging Writer's Contest
Open to writers of fiction, nonfiction, and poetry who have yet to publish or self-publish a book.
Prize: $2,000
Deadline: Entries open in March and are expected to close on 15 May, 2018
https://www.pshares.org/submit/emerging-writers-contest/guidelines
*

Fiction War Magazine's
Annual ATOM BOMB™ writing contest
Prize: $5,000 grand prize to a single work.
Deadline: May 30, 2018
https://www.fictionwar.com/2018ab
*

Fan Story Horror Story Writing Contest
Prize: $100 cash prize. All writers will receive feedback for their submission.
Deadline: June 1, 2018
http://www.fanstory.com/contestdetails.jsp
*

Flash Fiction Writing Contest

Write a flash fiction story that takes place during a hot summer night. Maximum length 500 words.

Prize: $100 cash prize. All writers will receive feedback for their submission.

Deadline: June 16, 2018

http://www.fanstory.com/contestdetails.jsp

*

Fan Story Faith Poetry Contest

The theme for this poetry contest is "faith", spiritual, political, intellectual or emotional faith.

Prize: $100 cash prize. All writers will receive feedback for their submission. Deadline: June 18, 2018

http://www.fanstory.com/contestdetails.jsp

*

Walt Whitman Award

The Walt Whitman Award is granted to an unpublished poetry collection.

Prize: $5,000, publication by Graywolf Press, and a six-week residency at the Civitella Ranieri Center in Umbria, Italy.

Submissions are accepted from September 1 through November 1 each year

https://www.poets.org/academy-american-poets/prizes/walt-whitman-award

*

3 annual Reed Magazine Contests

Entries open on 1 June and close 1 November.

John Steinbeck Award for Fiction:

Prize: $1,000. all entries are considered for publication.

Deadline: November 1, 2018

Gabriele Rico Challenge for Nonfiction:

Prize: $1,000. all entries are considered for publication.

Deadline: November 1, 2018

Edwin Markham Prize for Poetry:
Prize: $1,000. all entries are considered for publication.
Deadline: November 1, 2018
https://www.reedmag.org/submit
*

Bath Children's Novel Award
Open to novelists, of any nationality, who have yet to sign a traditional publishing deal for a novel. Any genre written for middle grade or young adult readers.
Prize: £2,000
Deadline: November 2018
https://bathnovelaward.co.uk/childrens-novel-award/
*

Annual ZOETROPE: All-Story Short Fiction Competition
The 2018 Short Fiction Competition opens July 1; for details, please visit the website; for updates by email, please contact contests@all-story.com.
Prize: $1,000. The winners and honorable mentions will be considered for representation by William Morris Endeavor, ICM, the Wylie Agency, Regal Literary, the Elaine Markson Literary Agency, Inkwell Management, Sterling Lord Literistic, Aitken Alexander Associates, Barer Literary, the Gernert Company, and the Georges Borchardt Literary Agency.
http://www.all-story.com/contests.cgi
*

Magic Oxygen Literary Prize
Prize: £1,000. Magic Oxygen also plants a tree for every entry in Boré, Kenya and will email entrants the GPS coordinates of the tree once they've received confirmation of the GPS coordinates from their Word Forest Coordinator.
Opens: 1st October 2018
Deadline: December 31, 2018
https://www.magicoxygen.co.uk/molp/

2 annual Bayou Magazine Contests

Contests Open: October 1

Contests Close: January 1

James Knudsen Prize for Fiction:

Fiction: $1,000 and a year's subscription to Bayou Magazine. Finalists will be named on our website, and all entries will be considered for publication.

Kay Murphy Prize for Poetry:

1,000 and a year's subscription to Bayou Magazine. Finalists will be named on our website, and all entries will be considered for publication

https://bayoumagazine.org/writing-contests/

Now that you at the end of this book, you are probably wondering, "Where should I start?"

*

Begin by revamping your marketing strategy with whatever activities you are most comfortable. If you an outgoing person, you should examine your book for ways to pitch your local TV station. Check a local event calendar for events you can talk about as an expert. If no fitting event is up in the next four weeks, check this calendar

http://www.holidayinsights.com/moreholidays/

Then, come up with a pitch and rehearse it in front of the mirror or videotape yourself. Go online, find your local TV station's website and check out anchors and producers. Compose a pitch and e-mail them. This is the same thing you would have to do if you hired a publicist, only if you did that you'd have to pay the publicist for finding the event and sending out e-mails.

*

If you don't feel ready for TV right now, please go back to

"… LIST A GIVEAWAY ON GOODREADS AND EVERYBODY WILL START TALKING ABOUT YOUR BOOK…"

Study this chapter again and join some groups at Goodreads (if you haven't already). Change your group settings so you can see the notifications best, and look for friends. Empower yourself by surrounding yourself with people who empower you because they believe in you and your work. Don't waste time by pursuing others.

*

If you need a change of scenery, visit your local Barnes and Noble store and browse magazines to see which ones you could pitch. The more articles you'll check out, the more ideas you'll have on how you can pitch your topic to the magazines. Be sure to note down all contact names or buy the magazines whose editors you want to pitch.

*

If you don't feel like going out – check out blogs or writing competitions.

*

This book began with a story how somebody who I had known for a decade teased and ignored me. And, how I had wasted time and money by pursuing this potential buyer again and again. All of us have similar stories to tell.

But, we are lucky – we live in the 21st century, where we are not confined to networking with the people who live in our neighborhood. We have opportunities to find and network with friends all over the world.

Without a doubt that is what will help you to save the most marketing dollars. I don't know if you know me or if a friend told you about my "naked books," meaning that I publish only books without fluff. But hopefully this book is proof that by listening to friends who share valuable information which costs only a few dollars, you are better off than listening to testimonials, which may not really show all facts at first glance.

If you found the information in this book useful, please share it with your friends. They will appreciate your input. Chances are they'll return the favor and share back information you did not know about. That is networking at its best.

Indie authors help indie authors! Together they make a dent in the universe of books!

ONWARD AND UPWARDS!

THANK YOU

for buying my book *Naked News for Indie Authors How NOT to Invest Your Marketing $$$ (2018).*

If you liked it please help your fellow readers and leave a review. To succeed indie authors need to know where they can learn best practices.

Hopefully, you'll connect with me

Twitter
https://twitter.com/Naked_Determina

Facebook
https://www.facebook.com/NAKED-Truths-Words-Elaborations-Determination-1415490208749151/

Google+
https://plus.google.com/u/0/103171286110985123907

Linkedin
https://www.linkedin.com/in/gisela-hausmann-03404913/

Web:
http://www.giselahausmann.com/contact.html

* * *

To find out about other 'naked (no fluff) books' that will bring positive changes to your life as well as special book deals

please subscribe at

http://www.giselahausmann.com/free-creative-ideas.html

Please know that this author respects subscribers and does not inundate them with sales emails.

* * *

Other books by Gisela Hausmann

NAKED TRUTHS About Getting Book Reviews in 2018 is the 4th edition of the only book penned by an Amazon top reviewer that shows you how you can "set the stage" for your book to receive authentic reviews and how to pursue getting them most effectively.

BAT SHIT CRAZY Email Requests looks at the topic from a humorous perspective. Also included is an analysis of the US presidential candidates' welcome emails' subject lines. It's a funny book but you can learn a lot from others' mistakes. (Paperback only).

NAKED GOOD READS How to Find Readers teaches indie authors how to use the best social media platform for authors. Amazon funnels all Kindle readers to this platform, now home to 65 million readers.

NAKED WORDS 2.0 The Effective 157-Word Email teaches best email practices in a 7-step system. This system is based on my work analyzing 100,000+ emails for effectiveness and personal appeal. The book helps readers in writing best marketing emails.

NAKED TEXT Email Writing Skills for Teenagers is the beginner edition of the above book.

The Little Blue Book for Authors Series presents essential knowledge:

The Little Blue Book for Authors: 53 Dos & Don'ts Nobody Is Telling You
The Little Blue Book for Authors: 101 Clues to Get More Out of Facebook

About the Author

Gisela Hausmann is the winner of the
- 2016 Sparky Award "Best Subject Line" (industry award)
- 2017 IAN Book of the Year Awards Finalist
- 2016 International Book Awards Finalist
- 2016 National Indie Excellence Awards Finalist
- 2015 Kindle Book Awards Finalist
- 2014 Gold Readers' Favorite Award
- 2013 Bronze eLit Awards

Her work has been featured on Bloomberg (tech podcast) and on NBC News (biz blog), in *SUCCESS* and in *Entrepreneur.*

Born to be an adventurer, Gisela has co-piloted single-engine planes, produced movies, and worked in the industries of education, construction, and international transportation. Gisela's friends and fans know her as a woman who goes out to seek the unusual and rare adventure.

A unique mixture of wild risk-taker and careful planner, Gisela globe-trotted almost 100,000 kilometers on three continents, including to the locations of her favorite books: Doctor Zhivago's Russia, Heinrich Harrer's Tibet, and Genghis Khan's Mongolia.

Gisela Hausmann graduated with a Master's degree in Film & Mass Media from the University of Vienna. She now lives in Greenville, South Carolina.

To subscribe to Gisela's Blog pls subscribe at
http://www.giselahausmann.com/free-creative-ideas.html

Gisela's website: http://www.giselahausmann.com/
Follow her at https://twitter.com/Naked_Determina

Notes:

Notes:

Made in the USA
Columbia, SC
10 February 2018